ENTREPRENEURGASM
33 Realistic Steps
Turning $1,700 into $103,000 Online
for the Average YOU

David Michael Ledesma

Copyright © 2014 David Michael Ledesma

Cover Layout by Jason Hudson

Cover Photo by Leo Kowal and gbh007

Printed in U.S.A.

All rights reserved.

ISBN-10: 1505311446
ISBN-13: 978-1505311440

DISCLAIMER, TERMS & CONDITIONS

The book's author does not make any guarantees regarding your future success and does not know your specific situation in both your personal and business life. Moreover, the author is not a lawyer or certified to give legal or business advice. By following anything in this book which may be interpreted as advice of any kind, you agree to do your own research and due diligence first and to take full responsibility for your own decisions and to not hold the author/publisher responsible or liable in any way for any of your actions.

If you need advice regarding your particular situation in your business and/or life decisions, you must contract an appropriate professional with whom you can interact with in person.

This book includes language which some people may consider offensive. Please stop reading if you are easily offended. For minors, parental guidance is advised.

IF YOU DO NOT ACCEPT OR AGREE TO THIS DISCLAIMER, YOU MUST NOT CONTINUE READING THIS BOOK. MOREOVER, IT IS SUGGESTED THAT YOU AVAIL OF THE DISTRIBUTOR'S 7-DAY RETURN AND REFUND POLICY, IF ANY.

DEDICATION

This is dedicated to all those who have tried and failed, that you may try once more and make it this time or the next (or even the next!); just like I finally have. You are not "trapped" in some world of failure (I know that feeling too; been there, done that). ENTREPRENEURGASMIC success really can and DOES happen!

ENTREPRENEURGASM

Table of Contents

Chapter I: Welcome!..9

Chapter II: Is Entrepreneurship for the "Average" YOU?...12

Chapter III: Let's Have an Entrepreneurgasm Together!..16

Chapter IV: **19 Steps of the Most Common But F***ed Up Business Plan**...........................19

Chapter V: **20 Myths vs. Facts About Modern Entrepreneurs**....................................24

Chapter VI: **6 Ways to Blast Away Business Risk**..76

Chapter VII: **33 Realistic Steps to Making Money Online**..92

Chapter VIII: A Free Gift for You! 128

ACKNOWLEDGMENT

I would like to thank all who have contributed and continue to contribute to this online world that has made so much success available to everyone else.

Chapter I: Welcome!

Hi, everyone! Welcome to my latest book about entrepreneurship.

Before anything else, I want to give you your FREE BONUS just for starting this book. To get it, **go to www.Entrepreneurgasm.com/Bonus** to download some really AWESOME stuff **including a PowerPoint slide presentation summary of Entrepreneurgasm**. What's more, you are allowed to use the PowerPoint slides for your own speeches, presentations, lectures and other stuff. Having that PowerPoint presentation on hand will help you breeze through this book even quicker. For best results, **go ahead and download it now before reading on**.

So why did I write this book? There are quite a few reasons. As some of you might already know, I wrote another best-seller in 2012 _Digital Marketing Madness: Social Media Marketing Strategy at Super Low Cost_ which talks on how to market your own business. There are probably some of you guys here who don't have a business yet. So where would you be applying all these marketing techniques? You might be applying it for somebody else's business or you might be applying it for a company that you worked for. But what about applying it to your own business, which might even be better?

Life is too short to be building someone else's dream

In my honest opinion, it's awesome if you are marketing for your own business or if you are making money for yourself and if you are working for yourself. Ironically, in this book, I will also be talking about how you might not necessarily have to work so hard even for yourself. However, I think it is even worse to work hard for somebody else and for somebody else's business and to build somebody else's dream. I like the saying that 'life is simply too short to be building somebody else's dreams;' so why not build your own dream?

Chapter II: Is Entrepreneurship for the "Average" YOU?

*(If you're already convinced entrepreneurship is for you, go ahead and **skip to Chapter III**, no guilty feelings!)* Are you cutout to have your own business? Is being an entrepreneur for you or is it not for you? We will talk about that in this book as well. I ask this question because some people just dismissively say that they are not 'entrepreneurial' or in some cases, other people tell them they are not entrepreneurial.

I remember a long time ago when somebody told me I was not "entrepreneurial" simply because I was not a careful and detailed person (I still hate "details," even to this day). I was very carefree and "unserious" with my life.

Other people, on the other hand, say they are entrepreneurial but then they fail because they don't really understand what "being entrepreneurial" really is. You ask them why they think they are entrepreneurial and **their basis is that they got flying colors when they took "online quizzes" on Facebook (haven't you?) or they believed hyped up media reports** about some entrepreneur somewhere with some great story and they say, "I want to be like that" or "I am like that and therefore I am an entrepreneur." Hopefully this book will clarify some of the misconceptions, more specifically about modern entrepreneurs.

I do believe that there has been a shift in entrepreneurial qualities from the past to the present. Not a big shift, but a significant shift. There are a lot of principles which are still very important and fundamental to entrepreneurship but there are a lot of things that may have been believed in the past which are really, really no longer true in the modern world; especially in this new age of the internet, social media, and the interactive web.

You might have gotten curious from the book's title; why do I mention $1,700 and why $103,000? The $1,700 is simple: that's my "guesstimate" of how much I invested in the early stages of my online business. As for the $103,000; for both privacy and legal reasons, let me just say that I am not in any way making any official declaration here. So IRS, if you are reading, please take note of that (wink, wink!). But let's just say that it is similar and based on "someone's" true story (wink, wink!).

I would also like to tell the IRS (just in case they are listening or reading), that I am not an American citizen nor am I an American resident. That being said, I think that $100,000 is very doable and realistic for YOU over a reasonable period of time. Now, what is a reasonable period of time?

It is different for different people. For some people who read this book, I would not be surprised if you can do it in **one year or even less**. For others, it might take you longer, **3 years, 4 years or 5 years maybe**, but within a **reasonable time** – definitely something to look forward to (let's put it that way).

The way it usually works from what I have "seen" is: it is normal that in the beginning you don't earn so much (maybe less than a hundred dollars a month or even zero) but then the earnings start to grow and grow. And by perhaps, the third year, you might (very realistically) be earning an **extra** $2,000, $3,000 or $4,000 a month.

Now, again that might not sound like much; only $2,000 or $3,000 or $4,000 a month but hey... you will see later on in this book that it is a realistic income **without** having to "work hard" or "work much" compared to common jobs, and without having to quit your job if you don't want to (Heck, wouldn't even $500 or $1,000 of **extra** income **without** much work be nice?). And that is even without having the usual hardships that people believe they have to undergo, so it is more about **extra** income.

After reading this book, I'm confident you'll be using and reusing it as a general guideline to start your business. Some of you may earn less than what I mentioned above, while some of you will earn way more than that. I dare say that for a LARGE NUMBER of you, **this book will be worth more than a million dollars** over your lifetime....

So **by the way, if you bought this online and finish this book within 7 days and you feel like you didn't get anything valuable at all from it, I encourage you to use the online book store's 7-Day Return and Refund Policy.** No worries and no hard feelings. I only appreciate your money if you find value in this!

Chapter III: Let's Have an Entrepreneurgasm Together!

*(Already believe in working "smarter" instead of harder? Just **skip** to next chapter!)* What is an Entrepreneurgasm? The answer is: it is **the great pleasure of starting up a business quickly** (without procrastination, no excuses of "I'm busy with other things right now," etc.), **as well as owning your own business and profiting from it**. Something will **always** come up making you "too busy," no matter what! If you continue to make excuses and say you'll "find the time" to startup your business "later," do you **honestly** believe you'll eventually find the time? Honestly! You know the answer to that.

Business is pleasurable for several reasons. One is that you are not working for somebody else; you are building **your** own dream. An entrepreneurgasm is also pleasurable because of the independence that you can gain as well as the income that you can derive from it. I think everyone has the right to this pleasure and I myself have experienced it and I want you to feel it too. Wow! So we'll both share an "entrepreneurgasmic" experience together, huh?

An entrepreneurgasm is not something for a "special" breed of people called "entrepreneurs" as you will see later when I go further. There are lots of quotes and clichés being thrown around on social media, especially on Facebook, Twitter or Instagram with feel-good images and sentences about entrepreneurship (Here's a stupid example: "Entrepreneurial success is 1% intelligence and 99% hard work").

Some of these "clever" quotes are true and great and I have experienced a lot of them myself, but quite a lot are really **not** necessarily true; but they sound great or look good on some cool background image. **The ones I hate the most are the quotes espousing the extreme value of hard work in aiming for entrepreneurial success.** Well, of course in anything you do, you need to "work hard." I mean, cooking dinner can be considered "hard work" for some people. Unfortunately, what these quotes often imply when they say, "You need to work hard to be a successful entrepreneur" is that you need to work harder than most other people and most other jobs. **You don't.** I completely disagree .

Of course, people can point to a lot of examples of successful entrepreneurs who work their asses off. I have respect for them. And guess what? I do believe that hard work **can** make an entrepreneur successful, but it is definitely not the only way to make entrepreneurs successful. There's more than one way to skin a cat! So why would you choose the hard way? I myself used to be a "victim" of hard work and when I say "victim" I mean I used to work really hard and earn a lot less. Later on, as a successful entrepreneur, I worked a lot less and earned a lot more. Beyond this example, there are a lot of false beliefs about entrepreneurs. So what is true and what is not true? I will go deeper into this later in Chapter V on "Myths vs. Facts about Modern Entrepreneurs." But first, let's look at the most common (and stupid) business plan which causes most "entrepreneurs" (including me) to screw up or FAIL their first business.

Chapter IV: 19 Steps of the Most Common But F***ed Up Business Plan

Do NOT fall into this trap below:

1. **Watch a TV program hyping up entrepreneurs.** How many of us have come across that?

2. **Decide that you want to be an entrepreneur too.** How many of us have watched a TV program hyping up entrepreneurs and suddenly decided, "Oh, I want to be entrepreneur as well."

3. Look around to see what businesses are already existing and decide which of those businesses you would like to also have.

4. **"Envision" yourself putting up a business just like one of those that you see.** ("Envision" is sometimes just a nice word of "daydream.")

5. **"Envision" your first customers coming to your imaginary business and liking it.**

6. **"Envision" your first customers telling all their friends about your business.**

7. **Imagine your imaginary growing customers.** Yes, "imagine your imaginary." I know that sounds silly but that's exactly what people do when they are "planning" their so called businesses.

8. **Imagine the media featuring a story about you and your growing market.**

9. **Be inspired by this imaginary vision and withdraw all your money, bet the house, borrow cash and look for investors among friends and family to invest in your dream.**

10. **Talk to friends about your business plan and get motivation from the ones who cheer you on... and ignore the ones who tell you its problems and challenges.** You may have heard quotes online as well which say that you should stick with positive people and "stay away from negative people;" and you may interpret that to mean that you should only listen to people who tell you what you want to hear. As a result, you may listen to people who say that your screwed up business plan is good and stop listening to people who bring you back to reality and tell you that it is wrong or that it won't work.

11. **Build and launch your business.**

12. **Start wondering why a lot less customers are coming than in your "vision."**

13. **Cling on to your dream. Watch and read more hyped up entrepreneurial media telling stories about entrepreneurs who almost failed but 'marched on' until they became billionaires.** Now I admit there are some of those people who did exactly that and they became very rich. But guess what? There are also a lot of people who bought the lottery and became very rich. Just because it worked for some people does not mean it is

probably going to work for most others in the same way. Later in the book I will talk about how to properly take entrepreneurial risks.

14. **Selectively look for the friends who cheered you to "go for it" and talk to them so that you can hear more motivation from them.**

15. **Continue to see your business fail.**

16. **Start getting desperate for cash and start cutting costs which often includes cutting quality, as well as start changing your dream business from a vision to a "quick buck" business just to try and keep it afloat.**

17. **Watch everything go haywire and get screwed up even more.**

18. **Start hiding from the money lenders, relatives, friends and everyone else that invested or lent you money for your dream business.**

19. **Lock up yourself somewhere and say "WTF just happened???"**

So what do you think of this common business plan? It is very real, isn't it? You have seen it happen or possibly it has happened to you already. I wouldn't be surprised. Well, guess what? A lot of it has happened to me as well. I don't blame you for it nor do I blame myself because it is really so common. So many people fall into this trap. Why? Because of the media hype and quotes that are thrown around on social media that they believe. So now that I have begun to bring you back to reality, let's look at the myths versus facts about modern entrepreneurs.

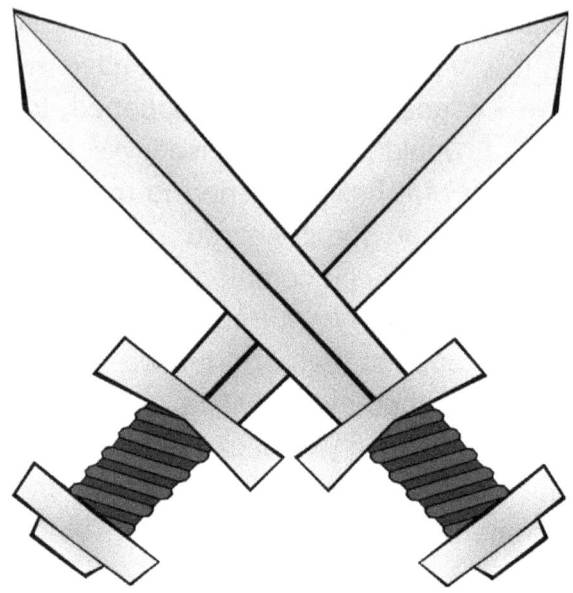

Chapter V: 20 Myths vs. Facts About Modern Entrepreneurs

I put together these myths vs. facts about (modern) entrepreneurs. Some are based on my own experiences and observations as a successful albeit small modern entrepreneur. On the other hand, some are based on interesting research I have come across over the years which seem to support my own personal experiences. Once you know these myths versus facts, you may be surprised to learn that you are cut out to setup your own business and experience your own entrepreneurgasm; and yes I am happy to experience that entrepreneurgasm with you and happy for you to experience that entrepreneurgasm with me, so we can experience our entrepreneurgasm together! So let's "get it on!"

1. Myth or Fact? "Entrepreneurs are born not made."

Answer: It depends. The truth is some entrepreneurs are born and some are made. They are not 'mutually exclusive.' When I say 'mutually exclusive,' I mean it doesn't have to be one or the other. Some people really are born entrepreneurs and seeing them makes you think that entrepreneurs are really born. Well, there may be 'born entrepreneurs' but **you** can still be 'made' as an entrepreneur.

A study was co-directed by Scott Shane, a professor of entrepreneurial studies at Case Western University, which compared entrepreneurial activities of more than 1,600 pairs of twins. They used twins in order to create some kind of "genetic control" because twins are supposed to have similar or even identical genes. The result? 60% of entrepreneurs are made and 40% are born.[1] So don't fret if you're

---

[1] Venture Atlanta. "Entrepreneurs: Made Or Born?" Venture Atlanta. October 21-22, 2014.
http://ventureatlanta.org/2011/09/are-entrepreneurs-

not part of the 40%. You can still be one of the 60% "made" entrepreneurs!

2. Myth or Fact? "Successful entrepreneurs are motivated mainly by money and about getting rich, and this is the main driving force of their success."

Myth. I disagree with this. I have two reasons; one is my personal experience, and the second is based on a study. So first, in my case: it was definitely not just about money. With my educational background, credentials, and connections, I could have earned a lot more money if I was willing to work in a company as an executive working my ass off; but still I preferred the entrepreneurial life because it gave me a lot of autonomy and freedom; and it allowed me to try and go for my dreams.

To corroborate this, I sight a Princeton University study[2] which suggests that entrepreneurs very often are motivated by autonomy and fulfilling a vision about their product or service that they want to offer to the public; and that getting rich is

---

    made-or-born/

[2] Lee, Alvin. "The entrepreneur's motivation: Not what you think..." INSEAD Knowledge. May 17, 2012. http://knowledge.insead.edu/innovation/entrepreneurship/the-entrepreneurs-motivation-630

very often a byproduct. Moreover, T2 Venture Capital's Jason Steiner made his own analysis of Dr. Cathleen Boss' study at the University of Minnesota on the psychological effects of money on human behavior. Steiner suggests that getting rich was just a byproduct[3] and that a lot of entrepreneurs are in it because they like the thrill of competition, desire adventure, and enjoy creating. We often assume that "being creative" is just for artists, but it is not. I think that great entrepreneurs are very creative people. They think of creative ways to offer their product to the public or they think of a creative product or service that they can offer the public. More importantly, as we'll see later on in this book, they think of creative ways to earn money by producing value or solving other people's problems.

Entrepreneurs and Finding Meaning in Life

Some entrepreneurs simply enjoy the satisfaction of team-building, and they feel that they are the ones building the team instead of just working as part of someone else's team. Other entrepreneurs go into entrepreneurship

---

[3] Steiner, Jason. "What Drives The Best Entrepreneurs? Hint: It's Not Money" Forbes. February 13, 2013. http://www.forbes.com/sites/groupthink/2013/02/13/what-drives-the-best-entrepreneurs-hint-its-not-money/

because they desire to achieve meaning in life. For a lot of you guys and gals reading this, be honest with yourself; how many of you feel that your job is meaningless and you are simply doing it for somebody else, to build somebody else's dream; or that you are just doing a job so that you can have money to survive? And... why are you surviving? So that you can go work. Why are you going to work? So you can earn money to survive. Why are you surviving? So that you can go to work. And so on. I mean, **how meaningless is that?** Entrepreneurs very often find meaning in life when they offer something unique or interesting to the public that nobody else is offering.

Entrepreneurs and Freedom

Earlier, I said that I enjoy entrepreneurship because I like freedom. It's the same for lots of other entrepreneurs. Now, I know freedom is a very big word and there are many kinds of freedom. **I classify freedom into three types:** financial freedom, time freedom, and decision freedom.

Financial Freedom

What is financial freedom? **Is financial freedom the same as being rich?** Well, not necessarily. I do not consider myself rich but I do consider myself "financially free." Financially free, for me, means being confident that I will have enough income and money to maintain my enjoyable lifestyle even without working my ass off or maybe even without working at all. I have some friends working for huge global companies who are earning very high salaries but who are working their asses off and they **can't** stop their work. If they stop working, they will lose everything. They will lose their good salaries and the lifestyle they are used to living. Does that sound like "freedom" to you?

In my case, I don't have to "work" in the sense that I don't really have to hold a day job because my online business earns enough money for me; my website earns by itself and I simply check it for 15 minutes once a day for a minor update, and then meet my web administrator for a more major update once a month (I have a trusted freelance web administrator because I'm not a tech guy by any means; so don't worry if you aren't one either!). So for me, THIS is financial freedom. Of course the ultimate financial freedom would be completely passive income where you don't even have to meet your web administrator once a month. Some people are born with such luck, such as "trust fund babies" from rich families. But even if you are not a trust fund baby like them (as I am not a trust fund baby myself), you still can achieve a huge degree of financial freedom following the steps I outline in this book

Time Freedom

Aside from financial freedom, there is also such a thing as "time freedom." This **is freedom to do what you like with your time or freedom to not do anything at all.** As already mentioned, I have a lot of free time because my online business earns money by itself and I just have to see my web administrator every month. Because of that, I have the freedom to do (almost) nothing and I even have to find ways to keep myself from getting bored. As a result, I have taken on two "hobbies." One is lecturing at university which I do because I enjoy it and it keeps me busy. The second hobby is film making. Some successful people play golf or spend their income on luxury cars. In my case, I don't really care for these traditional luxuries, but I do enjoy film making. Therefore, I end up producing my own shows for YouTube. My other passion is food; I love eating. To merge my filmmaking and eating addiction, I made a show which is about food; great combination, yeah? Again, these are just hobbies.

Decision Making Freedom

Another type of freedom is decision freedom; meaning you **have the freedom to make your own decisions regarding your own business and regarding your own life**... instead of having to follow the decisions of a boss or of a company that you work for. This is connected to the other two types of freedom above which I already spoke of in detail.

In a nutshell, a lot of entrepreneurs just want freedom more than money, and it comes in these three types of freedoms that I have just mentioned.

3. Myth or Fact? "Entrepreneurs are motivated to be 'entrepreneurial'."

Myth. I know this myth sounds strange, but why do some people become failed entrepreneurs? Because they simply want to be 'entrepreneurial.' They might read some story or watch some TV feature about some entrepreneur, and the documentary might hype up the characteristics of being 'entrepreneurial' and so suddenly they might say, "I am entrepreneurial" or "I want to be entrepreneurial and so I am going to setup a business tomorrow."

I'm sorry, but they got it wrong. You are not an entrepreneur just because you want to be "entrepreneurial." **Entrepreneurs are motivated by real world opportunity and not just by the thought of being an entrepreneur** as hyped up by the media. How do you spot these real world opportunities from which you can profit? It's easier than you think and I'll discuss this further in this book.

4. Myth or Fact? "It is best if your business is related to your passion."

Fact. According to a Brunell University study, successful entrepreneurs definitely tend to be in businesses which are related to their passion.[4] But take note, passion by itself is not enough. Just look at all the starving artists, painters, and unknown actors out there following their "passion." They may be so passionate about what they do, but they are not earning enough. So what are they lacking? Or better yet, **what do WE need, aside from passion, in order to be**

---

[4] Simpson, Ruth and Keith Dickson. "Emotional entrepreneurship: why passion + professionalism = success." Guardian News and Media Limited. January 30, 2013. http://www.theguardian.com/culture-professionals-network/culture-professionals-blog/2013/jan/30/emotional-entrepreneur-theatre-passion-profession

successful entrepreneurs? Simple, **we need 3 things:** passion, professionalism, and business acumen. You surely already know what 'passion' is, so I'll go through the next two in detail.

Professionalism and Business Acumen

The formal definition of professionalism according to Dictionary.com is "the standing practice or methods of a professional as distinguished from an amateur."[5] On the other hand, business acumen according to ft.com "is keenness and speed in understanding and deciding on a business situation."[6]

I have my own much simpler definitions. First, **professionalism means "getting things done, done on time, and done well."** Simple! Second, **business acumen for me is "the entrepreneurial ability to recognize opportunities, see how to profit from them, and take action."**

---

[5] professionalism. Dictionary.com. Dictionary.com Unabridged. Random House, Inc.
http://dictionary.reference.com/browse/professionalism
(accessed: October 30, 2014).

[6] http://lexicon.ft.com/Term?term=business-acumen

The reason why you see a lot of starving artists out there is that although they may be passionate or even professional, they don't recognize the business opportunities and how to profit from them. Some of them think that just because they have a beautiful painting, people are going to buy it. It's not as simple as that. On that point, there are also some business people who make that same mistake. Who are these business people? Product developers.

Product developers tend to have the misguided notion that just because they developed a good or even "awesome" product, people are going to pay money for it. For me, believing this is one of the BIGGEST reasons why "great" startups fail. You get a lot of hype in the media about people becoming instant millionaires when they opened up a startup (or more commonly.. getting millions in "funding"… which is NOT profit), but there are so many other startups out there with "great" products which are not earning money. Why? Because it's not as simple as creating a good product. Even if it's "awesome," that doesn't mean people are going to buy it.

Your Awesome Failure

This "awesome fail" phenomenon is not just for artists or product developers. Some so-called entrepreneurs are also like those starving artists. Why? They may be so passionate about their dream business such as, for example, a "cool" café. "Oh, it has been my dream to open a café." "It has been my dream to open a boutique shop." (And so on.) Then they spend money setting up these "dream" businesses and then because there is no market for it in their niche or their location, they end up losing money or going bankrupt. **There's a right way to follow your dream business, and there's a wrong way.** Later on in the book, we'll talk about how to make "dream" products or offer services that people will actually pay real money for, whether or not your product or service is as "great" as a lot of other hyped up startups' products.

5. Myth or fact? "You can spot a good entrepreneur when you listen to his or her great entrepreneurial ideas."

Myth. We often have that loud-mouthed guy among friends who always talks about entrepreneurship and entrepreneurial ideas (2nd place to the loud-mouthed stock "expert" dudes) and it is easy for us to think that he is a great entrepreneur, and that we are not as good as him. Well, guess what? There is a very big difference between talk and action.

A lot of real entrepreneurs don't talk about their entrepreneurial ideas simply because they are secretive of them. Why? They are afraid that other people will grab the opportunity before they do. Therefore, a true entrepreneur will often take action before talking. It is not talk, talk, talk and then action. Nope. It is action and then talk. Take action first and get your business off the ground and then you talk later on to try and bring people to your business. Not the other way around. So don't worry about those so-called "entrepreneurs" who just keep talking about these great ideas. You can beat them to the punch!

If you do have great ideas, don't talk about it yet. First establish a foothold or leverage before blurting it out to other people who could become your potential competitors. Make sure you are firmly in a good competitive position and you have power to win against competition before you start telling people about your business idea or about your business. Of course, there are exceptions because you may need to tell some specific people about your business; but you get my point.

6. Myth or fact? "The best followers make the best leaders, and the best employees make the best entrepreneurs."

Myth. This is soooo cliché. I always heard this especially from my primary grade school teachers because they wanted to make us work. You see, I was a lazy kid in grade school and high school. Moreover, I had quite a bit of a problem with authority then. So to get us students to follow them, our teachers would tell us these nice sounding clichés such as the "best followers make the best leaders" and B.S. like that. They sound good, don't they? And it is a great way to make kids follow. But sorry, I don't believe in this.

One characteristic of entrepreneurs according to a study by Ross Levine of the Haas School of Business at the University of California Berkeley and Yona Rubenstein of The London School of Economics, is that they tend to have aggressive, elicit and risk-taking tendencies as a youth.[7]

Does this sound like a good employee to you? Do aggressive, elicit, risk-taking people make good employees and do aggressive, elicit, risk-taking people make good followers? I don't think so.

Yet, according to the study, that is a characteristic of successful entrepreneurs. But take note, later on in this book I will also talk about how entrepreneurs may be "risk takers" but that does not mean they are "risk seekers."

So is being a good follower "bad?" Not at all. My take is that a leader is better if he or she was or is also a good follower, but being a good follower doesn't make you a good leader. There are good leaders out there who have never been good followers or will never be good followers but I think it helps if you can somehow have both qualities of a good follower and a good leader.

As mentioned earlier, entrepreneurs also tend to treasure autonomy and seeing their vision come to life. Quite too often, at least in traditionally-run companies, employees must follow the direction

---

[7] Burke, Adrienne. "Bad Teenagers Make Good Entrepreneurs, Study Says Yahoo Small Business Advisor." Yahoo Small Business Advisor. April 9, 2014.
https://smallbusiness.yahoo.com/advisor/bad-teenagers-make-good-entrepreneurs--study-says-174658106.html

and vision of a boss which may be different from the individual employees'. If you are an employee who is good at following a boss with a different direction and vision from yourself, how can you be the type who loves autonomy and also pursue your own vision? That is quite hard in a traditionally run company.

If you choose to work your ass off making somebody else rich

...why will you blame somebody else?

Of course, that is now sort of changing. It is becoming somewhat of a trend for some companies to give their employees a lot of autonomy, and a good example of that is Zappos which is run by Tony Hsieh. But generally, companies do not give this degree of autonomy and freedom to their employees. So if an employee enjoys an environment where he doesn't have much autonomy, then I don't see how he can be a good entrepreneur and I don't see how he can be a good leader either.

It can also be a disadvantage to be an employee if you get used to the "comfort zone." What's the "comfort zone?" This means you have become overly used to your life following the same daily routine as an employee and you don't want to step out of that routine "zone" to try something different and go for your dream and start earning money as an entrepreneur. Although not necessarily happy, we often become "comfortable" by almost automatically doing the same thing every day, day in and day out. Being in your comfort zone is one of the most **deadly** things that can prevent people from becoming successful entrepreneurs. As Sir Thomas Jefferson once said, "If you want something you've never had, you must be willing to do something you've never done." So get out of your comfort zone before it is too late.

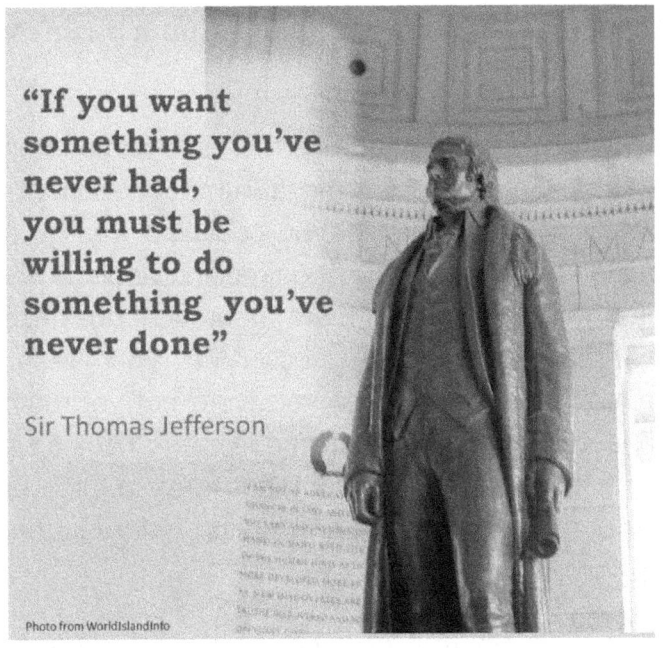

"If you want something you've never had, you must be willing to do something you've never done"

Sir Thomas Jefferson

Photo from WorldIslandInfo

What If You're an Employee Already?

Is having been an employee bad? Nope; in a way, it can help to have been an employee and therefore help you understand employees better. Look at it this way: IT skills can help you setup a restaurant because your restaurant has a computerized cash register system. Yet you can setup a restaurant even if you are not an IT professional, right? So it helps in a way to have been an employee, but it's not necessary.

7. Myth or fact? "The best way to become an entrepreneur is to work first as an employee

to gain experience and then setup a business later in life."

Myth. As far as I am concerned, this comes from another time. A long time ago, information was not easily available. All you could do was go to business school and in business schools in the past, you would often learn theoretical business, not really practical business. With your freshly minted business degree you were not yet ready to launch and run your own business. You had to work for some other company first to pick up experience in practical application before setting up your own business.

It is a lot different now because you can learn from the experience and mistakes from an infinite number of other entrepreneurs sharing their experiences online. Guess what? My most successful business had nothing to do at all with my past jobs. Did my past jobs help me at all in my current successful business? In a small way it did. How? If anything, my past experience as an employee taught me that I didn't want to be in those types of businesses where I had worked!

Weakest 1-word Business Plan

Aside from working for others, I also owned other businesses from which I garnered "experience." What happened to them? Either they failed or they just earned me enough to get by and they took up so much of my time, and I had to work so hard. On the contrary, my most successful business now had nothing to do with all of my past jobs. I learned it from scratch without any "experience" in this type of business. I learned it as I built it and I learned it as I ran it. Even more interesting… my most successful business is an online business and I'm NOT an

I.T. guy and I did NOT know how to "code" or do any technical stuff like that. I was just an average Joe who knew how to use Youtube and Facebook (just like you!), and from that, I made it happen!

My successful business which I have now came from thinking of something completely new and I had never done anything similar in the past (so again, it had nothing to do with my "experience"). In fact, that is part of the reason why it became successful. If my business was based on a past business which I worked for, then it might not be new. I would just be copying a business which already exists. How would my new business be differentiated from a past business?

A Different Kind of Experience

Don't get me wrong; experience is important but the best experience I got was not from working for some big company. It was from setting up my own small businesses and FAILING on my own and learning from those failures. So perhaps, you should start a business with complete psychological acceptance that it may fail; and take note that if it does fail, it will not be a worthless failure. It will be a valuable failure. In my case, I learned so much more from past failures and from my discontinued businesses than I learned from my previous jobs working for bigger companies.

Going back to the "entrepreneurial benefit" of working for a company as an employee first: **the bigger the company is where you work, the more worthless your experience can become!** Why? When a company you work for is very big, you get so called "experience" only from the department or section where you work rather than from the dealings of the whole company from a business owner's perspective. Also, big companies tend to let you gain experience in working with a big budget; a big budget you probably will NOT have when starting up your own business from scratch.

This is also a mistake in many business schools. The tools they teach you which you can apply in business mostly assume that you have a big budget to play around with; such as to launch an expensive marketing campaign, buy expensive equipment, purchase pricey computer or information systems, and the like.

As an entrepreneur, one of my best traits is to know how to achieve success while starting out with a tiny budget (all I had was my old, clunky laptop) and how to make use of all the best free resources we have online now, especially in this age of social media. I have seen, as a social media marketer and expert, how so many big businesses are earning big sales because they are spending so much on traditional marketing (i.e. expensive marketing) like TV advertising; but I see how they are failing miserably online and social media simply because they are doing it the wrong way.

Too often, their idea of social media marketing is to simply pay Facebook for Facebook Ads and to pay Youtube for Youtube ads when there is so much you can also do for free; such as creating "viral" videos or viral content which people online like to share and re-share, which spreads very fast.

I talk more about "viral" marketing in my other book *"Digital Marketing Madness: Social Media Marketing Strategy at Super Low Cost."* For this book, my point is that as an entrepreneur, you will be a lot more successful if you know how to achieve success when starting out on a small budget; and working for a big corporation very often does NOT teach you that. Instead, it teaches you how to spend a big budget which the Average You does not have!

8. Myth versus fact? "You need to work hard to be a successful entrepreneur compared to being an employee."

Myth. For me, this is one of the most annoying and irritating beliefs, quotes, and clichés being thrown around. Like I said earlier, working hard is relative and even cooking dinner can be "hard work" depending on how you define it. A better question about entrepreneurial hard work is, **"is it harder than being an employee?" My answer is NO.** This misconception comes from the fairytale assumption that the world is perfect and fair and that people are rewarded for working harder. Well, guess what? The world is not perfect. The world is not fair. There are a lot of people out there who work really, really hard. Just go to any third world country and you will see how some people are working so damn hard and earning so little. (By the way, I'm enjoying myself living in "3rd world" sunny Southeast Asia but I earn WELL and EASILY because my online business caters to the world.)

At the same time, there are other people out there who are hardly doing anything and are earning a lot of money; such as successful "netrepreneurs" who don't need to work hard. But I won't even use those guys as an example. I will use myself.

As mentioned earlier, I am by no means rich but I am definitely earning a very comfortable income working very, very little; just doing a significant update for my website once a month and doing minor updates a bit more often. You might say, "Oh, David had it good. David is lucky." Well, ummm... no.

In the past, I hated my work. I worked so hard and earned much, much less. Now, take note – **there is nothing wrong with working hard and it can definitely help you significantly but it is not necessary.** In my current successful business, maybe I went through a few overworked weekends where I worked like crazy but that happens with any job. In my case now, **I work 90% less than in the past and I am easily earning 900% more.** I repeat that: I work 90% less now and I am earning at least 900% more. It has nothing to do with the amount of work. From this I've learned that if you must always work more to earn more, then there's something wrong with your business model!

If you must always work more to earn more,

then there's something wrong with your business model.

9. Myth or fact? "Intelligence is needed for entrepreneurial success."

Fact. I will say this is true, but the question is, what do we mean by "intelligence?" Intelligence is needed for "anything." Even being an employee requires some intelligence. Even cooking dinner needs intelligence. So what is different about entrepreneurial intelligence?

Entrepreneurial intelligence is more specific in the sense that it is not necessarily about IQ and not about memorization of business textbooks. Entrepreneurial intelligence is about finding different, interesting and ingenious ways to solve problems. It is being observant and knowing how to spot business opportunities. It is being resourceful in knowing how to get the resources needed to launch your business. It is knowing where to get these resources, how to get them, and how to get them at a price that you can afford with your tiny budget. Finally, entrepreneurial intelligence is about learning how to lower or reduce risk; and knowing which risks to take and when to take them.

A while ago I said that **it is not true that entrepreneurs are risk-seekers.** A better description would be that they are risk takers. However, **before they are risk takers, they are first risk reducers.** They know how to reduce risk before taking it. They don't just carelessly look for risk and take it. A risk seeker in a casino is a gambler, and a risk seeker in business is a gamblerpreneur. That is not an entrepreneur. More on this risk aspect later.

10. Myth or fact? "College dropouts make better entrepreneurs than college graduates."

Myth (but yes, many dropouts DO make great entrepreneurs!). Again, this is very often hyped up in the media. Remember, the media likes to print great stories. They are not in the business of just simply delivering the best information. It would make quite a boring traditional story if you read about some A+ business school honors graduate who became a successful businessman.

It is a much more interesting and great story if you read about or watch a story about a guy who dropped out of college and became very successful. Because of that, we have lots of stories like these in the media, and we start believing that being a college dropout makes you a better entrepreneur. But that is a myth. **Some college dropouts DO become great entrepreneurs but a huge amount of remaining dropouts remain failures for the rest of their lives.**

The truth is it probably has nothing to do with schooling. A minority of dropouts become great entrepreneurs the same way a minority of college graduates become great entrepreneurs. However, college can provide some tools which make business more achievable, but it is certainly not a prerequisite.

According to research by Vivek Wadhwa in his work at Duke University, on average, companies founded by college graduates have twice the sales and employment of companies founded by people who hadn't finished college.[8] This suggests to me that if you do finish college, you are more likely to have a business which is twice as successful compared to a business of a no-college entrepreneur. But that does not shoot down the college dropouts either. Both can become successful entrepreneurs.

If you ask me, I think that if people have the determination to finish college, then they are probably more likely to have the determination to bull through the challenges of setting up their own business. Perhaps, the increased success is also because of the tools which are taught in college, assuming they went to a business school; or maybe it is because of the connections that they made when they were in college.

On the other hand, it is fair to say some great entrepreneurs really do have issues in school and I quote Richard Branson who said that "one thing that entrepreneurs have in common is a talent for seeing things differently. But this ability

---

[8] Wadhwa, Vivek. "Five myths about entrepreneurs." The Washington Post. July 29, 2011.
http://www.washingtonpost.com/opinions/five-myths-about-entrepreneurs/2011/06/29/gIQALtCBhI_story.html

often leads budding entrepreneurs to rebel against the conformity that is common in traditional education."[9] From what I know, Branson himself didn't finish college, so maybe he's biased and speaking from his own (super successful) experience rather than referencing successful entrepreneurs in general. I do agree though that entrepreneurs tend to dislike or even hate school; but that doesn't mean they dropout. In fact, persevering through college even if you hate it is a sign that you have the "grit to get things done" which is definitely a prized trait for real entrepreneurs (as opposed to useless "dreamerpreneurs").

So if it indeed is the case that entrepreneurs dislike or even hate school, I have created a graph just for it where we can compare the different types of people and whether they love or hate school; and whether they become achievers or whether they become useless people.

---

[9] Branson, Richard. "Richard Branson on Why Entrepreneurs Sometimes Struggle With Formal Education."
Entrepreneur. September 8, 2014.
http://www.entrepreneur.com/article/237034

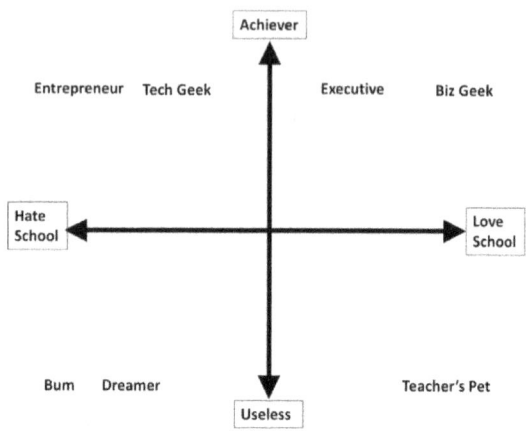

A warning from the graph: I would like to emphasize that there is a very strong similarity between an entrepreneur and a bum or a dreamer. So be careful because you might be acting like bum and then might not worry because you end up thinking, "I have entrepreneurial qualities because I hate school." Well, there is a very thin difference between an entrepreneur and a bum and it is very easy for a so called entrepreneur to fall out of the entrepreneur quadrant and end up as a bum. Which one do you choose to be?

Don't answer me with words. Answer with action. What action can you take so that you can be an entrepreneur instead of a bum or dreamer? Continue reading this book and I will discuss that in detail.

11. Myth or fact? "Good entrepreneurs are winners and not losers, successes and not failures."

Depends. It is a big cliché and there are quotes running around saying that failure is a great teacher. And guess what? I actually believe in this cliché. In my case, it has definitely held true.

My advice is to be "proactively ready" for failure. There is a difference between accepting failure as a quitter and being proactively ready for failure. How can you be proactively ready for failure? Contrary to the hyped up media stories about entrepreneurs who "bet everything in order to follower their vision," don't "bet everything you have" for your business. Bet only 10% of your available capital that you can afford to lose in the business. That way, you can afford to lose 10 times. Take note that in the amount that you can afford to lose, you should include one year of costs and expenses factored into your startup cost. That means you need enough money to let your business survive for one year even if you have zero sales. You might say, "God, that is a lot of money. It is so expensive to set up and to have enough capital even for just one business. How about ten businesses?" My answer: you can setup businesses cheaply. It is easy to do if you are doing an online business. I know that an online business is not for everyone so you might feel that this book is not for you. Well, whether you choose to do an online business or a traditional business, I think that there are a lot of principles in this book which you will find very valuable. You can simply ignore some parts of this book which are specific to online businesses if you wish. Just read on in this book and I will go deeper into this soon.

I would like to quote a meme being thrown around which is attributed to Robert Kiyosaki. He supposedly says that 90% of businesses fail so the recipe of success is to setup 10 business. I agree with that, but of course that doesn't mean setting up 10 businesses all at the same time.

12. Myth or fact? "You need to hire employees."

Myth. Again, with an online business you don't need to hire employees. Later on in this book I will tell you what kind of online business you can setup and that you also don't need to be a "coder" or an IT person. Some people think that they can't setup an online business because they are not IT people, or don't know how to do "HTML coding." Well, if you are in the food delivery business, do you have to be an auto engineer? I can argue that you need to be an auto engineer because you have to work on your delivery vehicles, right? Well, the answer is no. You just have to know how to drive the vehicles or you even just have to hire the vehicle drivers. It is the same with an online business. Your website is just a vehicle to deliver your product and services.

So how can you test if you are good enough to setup an online business or not? It is very simple: Do you know how to use YouTube? How about Facebook, can you use Facebook? If the answer is yes, then you probably know enough about online stuff to setup your business online, and you can learn more as you go along. You will be surprised how easy it is to do so much stuff yourself when you watch step-by-step tutorial videos. You can also outsource a lot of work to online freelancers via Elance.com, Odesk.com or Fiverr.com where many people are willing to do a lot of the work for you at reasonable prices.

13. Myth or fact? "Successful entrepreneurs are sociable people and need good public speaking skills."

Myth. I think this is a myth, especially in the modern sense, because if you choose to setup an online business, then you don't have to be very sociable. In my own biz, I don't even know my suppliers personally, and it doesn't really matter. I don't know my customers personally either. Heck, I even have online "partners" and affiliates who I've never met in person, but with whom I've been doing good business. When your biz is online, you can let your laptop earn money for you!

14. Myth or fact? "You need a lot of capital to setup your business."

Myth. There are different kinds of businesses you can setup. If you don't want to put up an online business, a service business generally does not need much capital. In my case, I did not need much capital because I setup an online business.

It is a myth as well that lower capital brings lower profit.

As for my story, I have owned 6 businesses. I've had 2 fast-food franchise restaurants, which is very high capital for an individual who is starting out. It earned "okay," a small profit and it eventually failed because fast-food is very competitive and labor costs are high. I'm sure you have seen on the news; labor costs may even go higher because there are a lot of protests being done by the fast-food workers.

I respect those fast-food workers. I do know that they work hard. If the world was fair and you based income on how hard work is, then yeah, they would earn more money. But because the world was not created that way, you don't earn more just by working harder. A guy digging on the street can dig and dig very hard, but that doesn't mean he is going to earn anything. My fast-food franchises were very high capital and required very hard work on my part as the owner as well; and they didn't earn as much as my current business.

Most people think that a fast-food franchise is easy to manage because the franchise already has the systems in place and other stuff. In reality, it is a business which is very hard to control because employee theft is a very big cost. Some ignorant business people tend to say that all you have to do is add a percentage to your cost and assume that that's how much will be stolen. Nonsense. Your people can steal anywhere from 1% to 50%. There is just so much room for theft by your own employees. You have to watch the business like a hawk. There is also a lot of stress because you have complaining customers and other problems. So it was high capital for me, a lot of work, for a modest income; and then eventually it failed.

I have also owned a tutorial school where I taught English conversation to Japanese housewives. That was moderately high capital because I ended up renting a real classroom. Moderately high capital for an individual, not as much as the fast-food franchise, but also medium to low income; it wasn't easy to earn money. It had very low expenses so I also didn't lose money but I didn't earn that much either; and it was a lot of work because I was personally teaching them myself and that takes up a lot of time.

Aside from that, I had one small sales distribution business for car accessories which was very low capital because I was simply distributing. I didn't really have to pay for inventory because I just had inventory on consignment, and the manufacturer was the one who bore the cost. But it also had quite a low profit. There were good months and there were bad months. It was also quite taxing on my part in the sense that I had to do a lot of work and I had to watch it very carefully as well to prevent theft and to prevent loss.

I also owned one advertising service (copywriting) business and was set up with moderately low capital but it was very hard work with long hours because I had to just keep working and working until my clients were satisfied and it only had small to medium profit. That was long hours and late into the night; sometimes I wouldn't even sleep at all. It was very, very stressful. Most people think that advertising is a fun business. There are a few fun aspects to it, but most people only see what is glamorized in the media and on social media when they see their advertising friends post the "extreme party life of advertising people." The reason advertising folks party so much is because it's so stressful that you go nuts!

And finally, I have had (and still have) one online business; extremely low capital (I guesstimate

$1,700 investment overall) and so far it has the highest and most consistent return as well as the lowest time investment on my part and the least amount of work – and extremely easy work.

So you be the judge: Which ended up the best for me? The high capital business or the low capital business? It could possibly be the best for you too (but of course, I don't know your exact situation).

15. Myth or fact? "You need a big budget for advertising and marketing."

Myth. It is **now** a myth because we have social media marketing which can be very cheap and effective if done correctly. For my online biz, I just started out on Youtube and then Facebook.

Youtube was the best, and it was free or can be free – but only if you know how to use it the right way. What is the wrong way? The wrong way to use Youtube for marketing is to simply make a traditional video advertisement for your business and then upload it to Youtube and then hope that people discover your video out of the millions and millions of other videos there. Guess what? Very few will see it. That is not how to use Youtube. Ironically, this is one way I see even giant corporations using Youtube. Even with their high-priced and "highly experienced" marketing "experts," they are simply uploading their traditional advertisements and hoping that people discover it. Funny thing about some marketing "experts" is that their price goes up when they have more experience. Problem is, their "experienced" price is high because of their "vast" experience in the pre-social-media days. Another reason is that giant corporations like to use expensive advertising agencies; and big ad agencies earn a bigger profit when the brand they're handling spends a big amount on advertising production and TV placements. What costs more to produce? A traditional advertisement for TV or a wacky home video which can go "viral?" Of course, it's a traditional advertisement which costs millions to produce and millions to place on TV. Is that bad? For the big corporations, maybe yes. For the "little guy" like you, it's a great thing! It allows you to compete with big giant corporations and WIN, even if you have a tiny budget.

Traditional advertisements are generally NOT what people would SHARE on social media. To succeed in Youtube, you don't make a video that people want to watch; you make a video that people want to **share**. And **what people want to watch is different from what people want to**

share. The same goes for Facebook, by the way: you don't simply upload a promotional poster of your product or service and hope that people will share it.

I talk about this deeply in my other book *Digital Marketing Madness: Social Media Marketing Strategy at Super Low Cost* but I will try giving you a "summary of a summary of a summary;" what makes people want to share?

The gist is that people want to share for "selfish" reasons. Huh? Yes. If you're a mother and you see a very useful video about how to clean the kitchen 80% faster and more effectively, will you share it on Facebook for other mothers to see? Yes. Why? Because you have a good heart? Perhaps. But the MAIN reason why you share it is you want to be "thanked and praised" by other mothers. See what I mean by "selfish?" Compare that to a traditional marketing video: you see a nice (traditional) advertisement about a product for mothers. It's a "nice" advertisement with a handsome husband, pretty mother, and beautiful baby. It even makes you smile. And then the product appears with the brand name. Nice. But will you share it? Probably not. Even if it made you "smile." Why don't you share it? Because you get no "selfish benefit" out of sharing it. Other mothers probably aren't going to "praise and thank" you for sharing it, so why bother? So now you see my point.

So the key takeaway is this: produce videos for Youtube and images for Facebook that people want to share, not necessarily what people want to watch or look at. They are different.

16. Myth or fact? "Before competing with the big guys you should compete with the small guys first."

Myth. On social media, you can beat the big guys (I have, on Youtube. Many of my business school tutorial videos are way up above those of huge universities). Again, I refer to the "selfish reason" why people share on social media which I talked about in the last myth above. Many big businesses don't seem to have a clue. They still create very expensive advertisements made for TV and newspaper, made by expensive and "creative" ad agencies, and then they upload it to social media thinking people will share it.

17. Myth or fact? "You have to be lean and efficient to be streamlined. You should only create or produce products and services which are being paid for and drop products which are not selling."

Myth. This comes from traditional marketing and traditional operations management where to be efficient, you only offer what people are buying. This is a myth, especially online. Online, one of the most powerful money-making business models is what we call "freemium" (free plus premium). You throw around a lot of free products and services, usually free videos or free e-books or free articles or free educational materials; and that attracts a lot of people; this is something that people like to share online. For example, a free video on how to do a good golf swing.

How do you make money? When people want to upgrade to your premium product or service, that's when you charge them. I will talk more about this later in this book. But the point is, unlike in a traditional business, you shouldn't carry just products that people are going to buy. You should carry both free products and premium products.

I do believe in the "lean" concept, but I do not mean "lean product line." I mean "lean" only with regard to operations and capitalization; and that you shouldn't spend much for marketing.

18. Myth or fact? "Either you choose a fun enjoyable business or a profitable business. You cannot have it both ways."

Myth. Well… of course if your only definition of a fun business is your dream café or your dream bar, then yeah, you could lose money or have a hard time surviving if your café or bar isn't a hit. But a business can be fun and profitable even if it is related to your passion. For example, if you have a passion for golf or you have a passion for makeup or cosmetics; or a passion for sports, then you can make your business related to that passion as long as you can also reduce risk.

Beware… you might say, "Oh, my passion is in cosmetics, so I'm going to setup a makeup store." There are already a gazillion other makeup stores out there with big brands; so of course you are (probably) going to lose. You don't just "set it up." You have to first reduce risk. Later on in this book I will tell you how to reduce that risk, because it is a huge topic in its own right and it would sidetrack us from our current focus on myths versus facts.

19. Myth or fact? "You need to drop your day job or give lots of your time and work a lot to earn more."

Again, this is a myth. This is called by many as the "time for money trap," where you have to trade time for money. You give more time so that you earn more money. Earlier in this book I already mentioned that. I said it is not true and I gave you my personal example where I earned a lot less when I was working a lot more. Again it is similar to the perfect world ideal and this is a "poor person strategy" where they give more of their time to get more money. The rich earn money to buy time. They earn money in more clever, efficient ways.

If my business delivers good value to you, regardless of whether I work much or not, you will pay me. Customers don't normally want to use a "time card" and pay you based on the number of hours you worked. They pay for what benefit they actually get from you. For example, I have an online tutorial business where people can watch my pre-recorded videos. Since it brings value to my customers because it **solves their agonizing problems** in helping them pass college or their MBA, they pay money for it.

On the other hand, if I am out on the street digging in the middle of nowhere working my ass off but it is not delivering any value to any set of consumers, will these consumers be willing to pay me anything? Successful entrepreneurs will find a way to deliver value and earn money from delivering that value. And what do they do with the money? They buy time. They can buy time in the form of not having to work, paying someone else to do work for them, extending their life through a "wellness" product, and/or just enjoying the day. Or perhaps they can buy time in the form of enjoying themselves on a good vacation. The point is successful people or rich people earn money to buy time. They don't have to trade (much) time to buy money. (Of course, a lot of successful entrepreneurs work a lot; but if you ask me, that's more out of choice.)

Do NOT fall into the "Time for Money" Trap

(Using more of your time to earn more money)

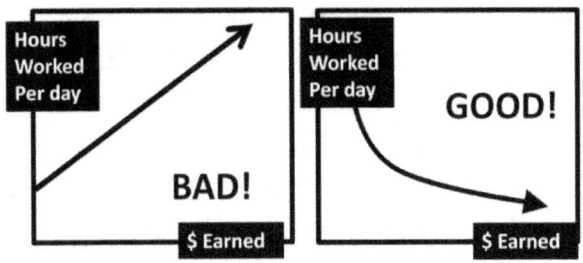

A good business model will let you efficiently increase sales and profit while using less and less of your time.

Later in the book, I will discuss how an online business can earn money by itself even if the owner (possibly you) doesn't work much. I live a very "luxurious" life. What do I mean by "luxurious?" Do I drive luxury cars? No, I don't. But I live a more luxurious life than many people who do. What is my luxury?

I found that great luxury is not about having a nice car, or staying in a five-star hotel when you are on vacation. I mention elsewhere in the book that I have some highly-paid friends who work in companies that book them in five-star hotels to attend seminars and stuff like that, but they don't get to enjoy it because at the end of the seminar, they are just so damned tired and they just crash on the bed. **The ultimate luxury is not having to wake up and go to work every day.** I can sleep the whole day if I wanted to. But I don't. Why? To keep myself from getting bored, I have quite a few hobbies. One of them is being a lecturer at university. But even without that job, I am all set with a comfortable lifestyle.

There is nothing wrong with waking up to go to work as long as you don't need to wake up to go to work. In my case, I enjoy my lecturer "hobby" and so I do wake up to go to class. So that is the luxury in my case, the fact that I can do anything I want in the daytime and choose any job I enjoy because I am not worried about the income; since my online business already provides it for me. On the other hand, if you enjoy your business, you could also **choose** to be both happy and busy at the same time. To represent this idea, taking into consideration both your happiness and "time freedom" with regard to entrepreneurship, I am showing you the Entrepreneurgasm Happiness Matrix:

Entrepreneurgasm Happiness Matrix

Bored	1) Unrelated to your passion 2) Virtual online business	1) Unrelated to your passion 2) Tangible traditional business
Happy	1) Related to your passion 2) Virtual online business	1) Related to your passion 2) Tangible traditional business
	Lots of Free Time	Busy

As you can see here, we can merge a happy life with lots of free time. You could also live a boring life with lots of free time or a boring busy life or a busy happy life. For me personally, the sweet spot is to have a happy life with lots of free time by doing something related to your passion in a virtual online business. As I say many times in this book, perhaps an online business is not your "thing." But even if it isn't, there'll still be a lot in this book which I hope you find interesting and enlightening!

20. Myth or fact? "High risk equals high return, and entrepreneurs are risk-seekers."

Myth. Again, this is "quick and witty" but otherwise stupid media hype. If you really believe that high risk is high return, then please drop whatever you are doing and go to the casino and try to get rich by gambling there. Obviously, that won't work out well for you. Entrepreneurs are risk takers, yes. That does **not** mean they are risk seekers. A good entrepreneur is a good risk manager, and a good risk manager knows how to reduce risk before taking it. He or she knows what the good risks are and how to reduce these risks.

There is a right way and a right time to take risks, as well as the right way and the right time to avoid risk. There is also the right way and the right time to minimize risk, and a right time to take risk. That is definitely not "risk seeking." That is risk managing.

In the past, I owned a fast-food franchise which required me to risk higher investment and which had a higher risk of failure. In fact, my first branch went unofficially bankrupt but luckily I gambled with a second branch which eventually paid for the debts of my first branch and then the first branch was eventually bought out by another franchisee. The second branch was successful for a time but I eventually had to discontinue it as well when tough competition started springing up nearby.

Now, my current business has risked very little capital. I just risked the cost of my laptop which was already a "sunk cost" anyway, and had almost zero risk of failure. When I say "sunk cost," I mean it was a cost I already paid for even before I started the business. I didn't have to make a special investment just for this business because I already had a laptop.

Eventually as I "upgraded" the business in the early stages (hiring a web designer, etc.) I guesstimate I capitalized it with only around $1,700. How did I reduce the risk of capital and how did I reduce the risk of failure? That brings us now to the next chapter.

Chapter VI: 6 Ways to Blast Away Business Risk

First of all, let me say that **there are two types of risk**. Risk is often mentioned as a general term but I classify it into two types and we have to think of both these types so that we can reduce each of them. The first is **"risk of failure"** and the second is **"risk of losing capital"** or risk of losing the money you invested in your business. Now that we're clear on that, let's talk about both these types of risks individually.

Low Risk versus High Risk of Failure

How do you reduce risk of failure? It is actually very simple. The best way to have low risk in business is to "solve the unsolved problems" of a market that has money to pay you. If you can solve the unsolved problems of others, then it is almost sure that those others are willing to pay you to solve their problems for them. The bigger the problem you're solving, the smaller the risk. If you're solving a giant problem, your business will be almost zero risk (maybe even smaller than the risk of getting fired from a 'safe and secure' job!). That's why a medical company earns money.

Even if people do not want to buy their products (who likes taking medicine? Bleckh!) and even HATE medical treatment and HATE medicines and HATE medical companies, people still pay them and medical companies still earn money. Why? Because these medical companies are solving problems for the people. When people are sick, that is a problem or a big problem which MUST be solved.

Risk Reduction Tactic 1: Solve unsolved problems of a market which has money.

One common misconception among businessmen and marketers is that the only way to make people buy products is to make them want products. That is one way to do it, but that is not the only way and it is not necessarily the best way; and it certainly is not the lowest risk way. In fact, it is risky in a way because even when people want your product, that doesn't mean they'll buy it. How many things have you seen something online that you "super want" but haven't bought?

Why haven't you bought them? You might say it is because you "cannot afford" them but in reality it is because they are not solving your problems or they are not solving big enough problems for you to need it. If you are sick and you are in the hospital and you are dying and the medical cost of that is the same as an expensive car which you say you "cannot afford," believe me, you will find the money somehow and you will pay it, right? So the "affordability issue" is not what is preventing you from buying stuff you "want" online; it is because a lot of this "stuff" is not solving your problem.

You might say, "David, you're wrong! Expensive car companies are earning money and profits!" Yes they are and I will talk about that more in detail later in this book. I am not saying that solving people's problems is the *only way* to earn money. There are other ways to earn money such as selling stuff in the luxury market; but I am simply saying that the *lowest risk* business you can setup is one which solves other people's problems. You might tell me that there are some drug companies which lose money. True; but it is because A) they weren't really solving consumer's health problems or B) maybe some other drug company was already solving that problem for consumers and so they are just coming in to a market which already has competition. I stated earlier that "solving an **unsolved**" problem was the lowest risk.

Loser vs. Entrepreneur

Loser:
"Look for others' problems to join complaining about it."
Entrep:
"Look for others' problems to make product solving it."

Low to Medium Risk of Failure

How about <u>low to medium risk?</u> The best example of this is meeting the demand of non-problems. So there might not be a problem but there is a demand for it, or perhaps an existing demand for it, which is not yet being served.

> Risk Reduction Tactic 2: Meet demand of non-problems.

For example, you are in an area with many Chinese students who you know have been looking for a Chinese restaurant to eat at regularly, but there is no Chinese restaurant there yet. There is a demand for Chinese food that people are willing to pay for but that demand is not yet being served. So if you were to set up a Chinese restaurant here, then that is relatively low risk. Not as low risk as solving problems but it is still quite low risk or low-medium risk.

Medium Risk of Failure

Next in line is medium risk. You encounter medium risk when supplying what others already probably want.

In this case, you are not 100% sure they would want it but you think they *probably* would want it;

or maybe you are sure that they would want it but you are not sure that they would actually pay for it.

> Risk Reduction Tactic 3: Sell what people probably want.

An example would be an improvement to an existing product. So maybe you already see the product in the market and you think you can make it better; so you setup a business selling your "better" offering. Like what? It might be a more delicious burger, better software, a more comfortable type of clothing, and the like. With this kind of thing, it is not yet very high risk but it is definitely not low risk anymore. This is already a moderate gamble because it is not very sure. Even though your burgers are more delicious than an existing burger in your neighborhood, it doesn't mean that people would actually shift to you. But it *might* be worth the risk.

A variation of this business model is supplying an existing product at a cheaper price than the competition. However, I advise against this as it can result in a price war that can drive you to ruin and failure. This is a very common business model I see around; you may say, "Wow, somebody is selling something at this price so if can sell it cheaper, I will earn money for sure."

However, once you get into that business, the existing guy who is already there can also lower his price to compete with you and then suddenly, you have lost your market. If you lower your price again, then he can just lower his price yet again; and then you end up with a price war and both of you lose. But most probably, you will lose quicker than he will because he has already been in the business for some time so he already has some customers who are comfortable buying from him who will not shift to you; or because he has been in the business longer, he has already been earning money for a longer time and so he already has the capital to continue the business at a lower profit margin than you. In your case, you are still starting out and you have to pay for a lot of costs such as your startup costs and other stuff.

A Business with High Risk of Failure

Even higher or possibly having the highest risk of failure would be to come up with a new product or concept that others **might** want. So for example, you say, "There is already the Android. There is already the iPhone." And you decide to come up with the first generation "ZIYN Phone." You may have read the hyped-up stories about Steve Jobs about how he created his product for consumers who "didn't know what they wanted until they saw it" and you say, "I am gonna be the next Steve Jobs." Deep inside your mind what you're really saying is, "I want to be like Steve Jobs." even though you are not him. This is a great dream and it can possibly make you super-duper, uber-rich. However, please do understand that this has extremely high risk of failure. This is almost as risky as a lottery ticket.

So if you do this and you do become successful, please don't come back and blame me and say, "David, you we're wrong. See? I'm the new Steve Jobs!" No, I am not wrong. I am right. If you do become the next Steve Jobs, I admire you! But in terms of risk from your viewpoint today, my best advice is that this is extremely high risk and I do not recommend it as your first business. Perhaps in the future when you already have a good cash flow coming from your less risky business, you can venture into a high risk ZIYN-Phone or something like that. But not yet right now.

So among the four types of failure-risk I mention above, which is best for you? Well, for me, it is quite obvious. It is the first one. Try to solve unsolved problems for a market which has the money to pay you to solve problems.

Of course, another factor to consider is the amount of money ("purchasing power") your target market has. To take this into consideration, I've created the Entrepreneurgasm Risk of Failure Pyramid:

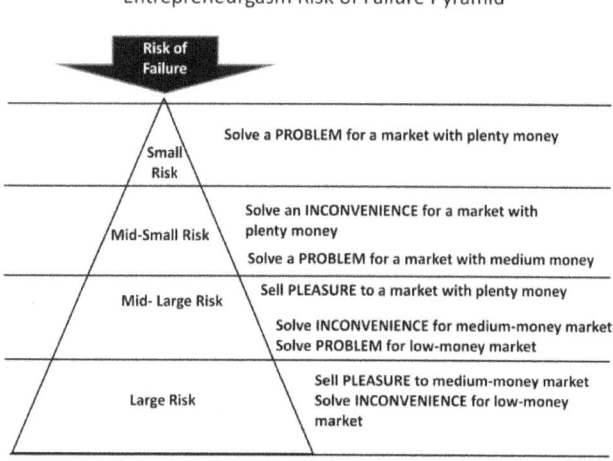

Entrepreneurgasm Risk of Failure Pyramid

In the pyramid above, we demonstrate what businesses you can put up from small risk to large risk of failure. To complete the idea mentioned earlier: the smallest risk is to solve a problem for a market which has money to pay you. Medium to smaller risk is to solve an *inconvenience* for a market with money. Selling pleasures (or luxuries) can earn money too, but they are higher risk.

For example, you notice that people are walking more than 500 meters just to buy water in your apartment building and it is a big inconvenience for them, but it is not a problem. If you solve that inconvenience for them by setting up a water vending machine in your apartment building, then that is small to medium risk. You are almost sure people are going to buy from it. Or alternatively, it would be small to medium risk to solve a problem for a market with less money; because even if it solves a problem, it does so for a market with less purchasing power.

To reduce risk even further, try to solve problems or inconveniences in a way that is hard for your competitors to replicate or duplicate. We call this "inimitable" or "not easy to imitate." You might solve a problem that people have, but the way you solve it is with something which is very easy for competitors to copy. If they can setup shop in one day, you might not be successful either because suddenly, you might have 100 other competitors jump in the moment they see you earning good money. Look at the "selfie stick" which became common in early 2014 (go ahead and Google it if you don't know what it is). It solved a (small) problem or inconvenience for selfie-takers whose arms weren't long enough. It did sell a lot; but look at how quickly competition was able to make almost exactly the same product and compete with the inventor. Heck, I don't even know which inventor or company started it... competition jumped in so quickly and easily that the inventor or original company wasn't able to build a brand fast enough.

> Risk Reduction Tactic 4: Sell a product or service which is hard to copy or imitate.

Moving on to medium to large risk, you can sell "pleasure" to a market with a lot of money. This is where the luxury market comes in. This is why jewelers earn money even though they are not exactly solving problems. They are selling pleasure to high income and wealthy people. If you do that, are you going to fail? I have no idea, but it is definitely medium to large risk for you.

Was it medium to high risk for these jewelers who are earning good money? It was medium to large risk for them maybe when they first started, but no longer is because they already went over their "risk hill." From the pyramid above, we see that there are so many combinations. So even if you are solving a problem it may still be medium to large risk if you are doing it for a market which does not have much money to pay.

Risk of Losing Capital Investment

We have already discussed the risk of failure. How about the other type of risk? The risk of losing money or losing your investment?

The highest risk of losing your investment comes from setting up a traditional tangible business with a tangible product and tangible office or shop. When I say "tangible," I mean it is something you can touch, see, and feel. This is a high risk investment because you have to invest in an office, you have to invest in your factory, you have to invest in a restaurant and other tangible stuff which costs a lot of money and so you risk losing that money.

For a lower risk of losing money, you can make a traditional tangible business which offers human service rather than products.

You invest less money in this. You might just need an office and some facilities and then some service people who you might pay based on work done. You don't have to spend much on inventory, plant, property and equipment, and instead just spend on salaries (if you have any employees), or on yourself (if you're still starting out and doing the service yourself).

> Risk Reduction Tactic 5: Set up a service business.

Now, if you want an <u>even lower risk</u> of losing money, then I would recommend creating a virtual information business online like what I have. With this one, all you need is your laptop which you probably already have and need to spend on some software if you don't have it yet; of course, you also need a good internet connection.

With this type of business, if it fails, you don't really lose much. You just lose the price of a laptop (if you didn't have one yet) and the cost of the software. Perhaps you lose the money you spent on your internet connection, but I'm sure you already have that one too. Probably the biggest amount of investment and potential loss comes from website development which is still very small compared to investing in a traditional business.

> Risk Reduction Tactic 6: Set up a virtual information business.

To get a better overview of capital risk, let's take a look at my Entrepreneurgasm Risk of Capital Pyramid:

Entrepreneurgasm Risk of Capital Pyramid

Small Risk	Virtual Business (Online), Information Business, Home Businesses
Mid-Small Risk	Service Businesses or "Guerilla" Type Businesses (Food truck, Coffee Kiosk, etc.)
Mid-Large Risk	Small Tangible Business (Restaurant, Café, Boutique, Spa, Book Shop, Print Shop, etc.)
Large Risk	Larger Tangible Businesses (Larger or Chain of Restaurants, Factory, Resort, etc.)

I've outlined the smallest risk to the largest risk businesses with examples. Of course, you may have a cross between these businesses above. Maybe you might have an online business which delivers or sells tangible products, for example. But it is good to at least know and think within the structure of my Entrepreneurgasm Risk of Capital Pyramid so that you can make a better, more informed decision.

An Overview of Business Risk

Let's merge what we just learned about risk. There are two types of risk: risk of capital and risk of failure, which I have represented in the Entrepreneurgasm Business Risk Matrix.

Entrepreneurgasm Risk Matrix

High Failure Risk	1) New information product concept	1) New service concept	1) New tangible product concept
Medium Failure Risk	1) Supply what others will probably want 2) Virtual online business	1) Supply what others will probably want 2) Service business	1) Supply what others will probably want 2) Tangible products/store
Low Failure Risk	1) Solve unsolved problems 2) Virtual/Info product 3) Supply un-met demand	1) Solve unsolved problems 2) Service business or app creation	1) Solve unsolved problems 2) Traditional tangible business
	Low Capital Risk	Medium Capital Risk	High Capital Risk

We see in the matrix businesses from high risk of failure to low risk of failure, and high risk of capital to low risk of capital. From this you can choose what type of business you might want to startup depending on the type of failure risk you are willing to take and the type of capital risk you are willing to take. Obviously, the best choice if it is available to you is to choose a business which is both low in risk of failure and low in risk of capital. Therefore, my bias is to solve other people's problems using a virtual information product and to supply unmet demand. If you truly feel that an online biz isn't for you, I fully respect that and I'm sure there's still a lot in this book which you will find valuable. On the other hand, if you wish to follow my lead and are interested in setting up your own online business, you are now ready to move to the next chapter of the book on 33 Realistic Steps to Making Money Online.

Chapter VII: 33 Realistic Steps to Making Money Online

Finally, we go into the realistic steps to make your entrepreneurial dream come true, based on everything we learned in the book up to this point; whilst avoiding the common screwed up business plan which we talked about earlier. We reach for our goal while lowering capital risk, lowering failure risk and increasing probability of success.

I am letting you know in advance that there is definitely an online bias in these steps because as we learned in the previous parts of this book, it really seems to be the best way to have low capital risk and low failure risk. It is extremely easy to setup even with minimum resources. If an online business is really not for you, then I am sure you will still find some wisdom in a lot of the concepts discussed here which you can apply even to a traditional business. That being said, I really would ask you to at least consider an online business and quickly browse through this chapter. Afterwards, if you decide it's not for you, no worries. Let's go right to the "steps."

Step 1: Think about your passion.

Remember, Steve Jobs had a passion for computers, as did that dude Amos of Famous Amos cookies. You might have a passion for photography or passion for the beauty industry or passion for golf or something else. I did say you may not be the next Steve Jobs, but that is okay. We will account for that in the coming steps.

Step 2: Think about problems of people within your passion's niche.

It is not as simple as selling cosmetics if cosmetics are your passion. It is not as simple as selling golf clubs if golfing is your passion. It is not as simple as selling cameras if photography is your passion. Instead, think about the **problems** experienced by other people in your passion's niche. If you are active in your niche, you have probably experienced many problems or inconveniences yourself. Think about problems or inconveniences of people in that niche which have not yet been solved. What are the unsolved problems in your niche, or at least in your location? (Could be geographical location or even virtual location.)

PRO TIP: Read the **online forums** related to your passion. There you will find a multitude of people in your niche voicing out their unsolved problems (in the form of questions).

Step 3: Think of how to solve these problems.

Pretty simple. It may not be easy, I admit, but it is simple. This could take a few of days, but think about it. How could these problems be solved? Make a whole list. Careful; if you're taking more than a couple of days then you're probably "drifting" away from the entrepreneurial mindset. Knock yourself on the head and make "problem solving" a habit, just like it's a habit to drink coffee or tea every morning.

"There's an infinite number of problems in this world...

...you only need to solve <u>one</u> for the right market"

Step 4: Think about how to solve these problems online.

Once you have made a whole list of how these problems can be solved, think about how to solve these problems online.

There may be many ways you can solve it online. Maybe it could be solved with the use of apps. It could be solved with the use of software. But the simplest non-technical way to solve it online, if you are not a tech-geek, is to solve it using information. What information? Think of how to solve it "your way" and document that information or record that information which you can make into videos and e-books. We will get into that later. But the thing for now is to simply think of how to solve it online.

Step 5: Think of how you can charge money for solving these problems online.

When we talk about earning money online, we call this "monetization" (money + tization). Earning money online is not just about "getting advertisers for your website." You will probably earn very small money from advertising. Even if you have a successful website with thousands of visitors a day, you probably won't earn much. According to anecdotal evidence which I cannot verify (because of confidentiality policies), even if you have a thousand views a day on your website and you are earning money from banner ads or text ads, you might earn $2 or $3 a day. Therefore, you have to find ways to earn money from your website aside from advertising.

Think of other monetization options which fit your niche. For example, you may sell your own tangible products. Up until now, I was recommending that you sell information products. But yes, you may also sell tangible products online. If you are an IT person or you know an IT person who can develop apps or software for you, you can also sell electronic products.

You can also sell affiliate offers. So for example, you might not have your own information product (such as a downloadable PDF e-book). You can go to a website like JVzoo.com which is a very big affiliate network and look for an e-book which you think your followers might be interested in and you can promote that e-book on your website. How does it work? You promote an e-book from another author who you found on JVzoo.com and if your followers or fans click on the "advertised" (actually "affiliated") product on your website, they will be redirected to an external separate website which is selling that external e-book. If a purchase is successful, then that other website will automatically share commission with you of around 50% which is very big compared to other famous online distribution companies. How do you make sure that the other website/author pays you? No worries, JVzoo will take care of it. Note that JVzoo is not the producer of that other e-book. It is just a network which brings different website creators like you together with other product creators and it works as a system in between you guys to make sure that you get your affiliate commission for promoting other people's stuff.

Another way you can make money online is through personal coaching, consulting and tutoring. Although this can bring in good cash flow, I do not recommend it for the long term because like I said earlier, I prefer a business system which allows you to earn money with very little work. If you are coaching and consulting then it is going to take up a lot of your time. But if you are still starting out, then you may want to do it just to bring in some cash to survive. If you do allow this for the long term when you are already "famous," you can accept personal coaching and consulting gigs only in exchange for very high fees, so that it is really worth your time. You will be surprised when you already have lots of followers and fans. Even a small percentage of them might be willing to pay you for coaching and consulting online for lots of money. How and where will you find lots of fans and followers? Read on, I'll get to that soon!

For me, by far the most powerful online monetization model has been the "freemium" model (free + premium) which I already talked about briefly elsewhere in this book. In the coming steps, I'll give you an example of exactly how you can do this for your own biz.

Step 6: Draw Your Own Entrepreneurgasm Business Ball.

I created this Entrepreneurgasm Business Ball to help you decide what you want to do related to a low risk, low capital investment, with low work commitment and high success. It is all about merging risk minimization, profit maximization, and passion.

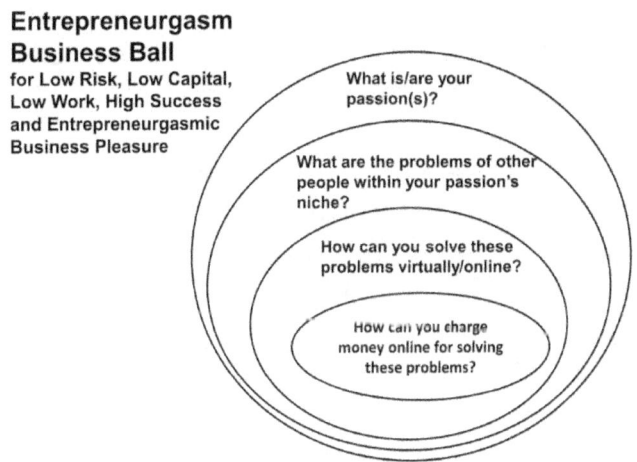

How do we use this? We solve big problems for people connected to your passion by providing information from an online business with very small startup cost and tiny expenses. Feel free to share this Entrepreneurgasm Business Ball with your friends. You can download this image from my website and feel free to share it or use it in your own presentations or publications, as long as you give proper credit.

Step 7: Think of a business name which can also be your website name, your YouTube name and Facebook fan page name.

You have to check all of that together and make sure it is all available. Make sure the "domain name" or web address is still available. Make sure your YouTube name is still available. Make sure the Facebook fan page name is still available.

(I have a secret free resources page on my website with videos which will help you to do this. How can you find that secret page? I'll talk about that in Chapter VIII.)

Make sure this is a memorable catchy name but it should not have any confusing spelling or apostrophes or punctuations because that can really mess things up when communicating your web address and communicating your fan page. Preferably, it should not end with an "s" in the end or should not easily be mistaken for having an "s". For example, "BestSolution.com" can easily be mistyped as "BestSolutions.com. Or "SolutionsService.com" can easily be mistyped as "SolutionService.com" (the customer may not realize that there's more than one "s" in the middle). If your business name is something like "Harry's Business," this can be confusing as well. Your web address may be HarrysBusiness.com without an apostrophe but some consumers will mistype this as Harry'sBusiness.com which will give them a dead link. You get my point.

Step 8: Setup your YouTube account. This is easy to do.

(I have a secret free resources page on my website with a video which will help you to do this. How can you find that secret page? I'll talk about that in Chapter VIII.)

Step 9: Reserve your Facebook fan page name. No need to design the page yet at this point. Just register it with your chosen name.

(I have a secret free resources page on my website with a video which will help you to do this. How can you find that secret page? I'll talk about that in Chapter VIII.)

Step 10. Buy your domain name, also known as your web address. For this, you can just use a common register such GoDaddy.com.

(I have a secret free resources page on my website with a video which will help you to do this. How can you find that secret page? I'll talk about that in Chapter VIII.)

Step 11. Create and design your Facebook page.

(I have a secret free resources page on my website with a video which will help you to do this. How can you find that secret page? I'll talk about that in Chapter VIII.)

Step 12. Start making your website.

Now, here's where it gets a little bit technical. If you don't want to go through the technicalities of it and you are low on budget, then I do not recommend going to a website design "company." The lowest cost way is to look for a freelance student to do this for you, and make sure he uses WordPress. Why WordPress? Once your web designer sets it up, it will be easy for you to manage on your own (with a little training) even if you're not a technical person. I prefer if you have a friend refer somebody to you because if this freelance student eventually becomes your web administrator, this is somebody you need to trust. This is not somebody you will need working for you fulltime.

You just have to see him every once in a while to help you update your website but it is still somebody you need to trust because you are not just making a website for fun, you are making a website for business.

Your web admin can screw you over if he wants to. For example, he can steal your content or videos; and there are ways he might be able to funnel online payments on your website into his account instead of into your account.

You can also try making the website yourself. If you do, I recommend OptimizePress or Instapage. With a little practice, these are both programs which are very easy to use. They are drag and drop. They are almost as easy as using Microsoft PowerPoint or maybe even easier (I'm sure even you had some difficulty using Power Point the first time). You should afterwards install WishList Member. WishList Member is a "plug-in" which will allow people to register as members and enable them to pay your membership fees so that they can access your premium videos (more on premium videos later).

It is also around this time that you can experiment "broadcasting" your website to cyberspace via a "hosting account." Your web admin should know how to do this. If you're just starting out, you can use GoDaddy.com's hosting service. If you bought your domain name (web address) through GoDaddy, they even have a free hosting service but I do NOT recommend it. If you don't want to spend too much, go with a $5/month low-cost hosting plan (in the meantime), but do not get the free, unreliable, slow hosting package.

If you want to lessen your risk of capital investment, you may choose to setup your website and do all of your website steps <u>later</u> if you wish, after you have already collected lots of social media fans and followers that you can sell to. That way, you are only spending money in setting up your website after you already have a base of fans and followers. However, if you are willing to take the risk (it doesn't cost much compared to a traditional tangible business), then it is better to set this up early so that you already have an existing website from which you can sell to your first batch of fans and followers. When you get fans and followers even for the first time, it is a waste if you can't sell anything to them just because your website isn't up yet.

OptimizePress and WishList Member are not free but they are very reasonably priced. They are about $100 each so that's only $200, still way below the $1,700 "psychological budget" which I recommended in the title of this book. Even if you use a freelance student, he probably wouldn't charge that much just to setup a WordPress site. He might cost you not more than $500 (perhaps offer him around $300 first and then pay him more as you go along, as I'm sure you'll want a lot of additions and revisions).

Step 13: Setup a PayPal "Premier" account.

Maybe right now, you already have a PayPal individual account or even a PayPal verified account; but that individual PayPal verified account does not allow you to accept payments the way a business can. If somebody wants to pay you online or somebody wants to pay you through your website using a selling tool such as a "buy now button" or with his credit card, you will need a Paypal Premier or Paypal Business account.

A customer won't be able to pay that into your PayPal individual account. A PayPal Business account is slightly better than a PayPal Premier account in the sense that it will use your business name rather than your personal name, but it is also so much more complicated to setup. I would say that if you are just starting out, a PayPal Premier account is more than enough.

Step 14: Make free videos.

Make and record your free information videos related to your niche, preferably about solving problems. There are many tools you can use for that. You can just use your laptop camera if you want and some Youtube examples are BubzBeauty, Michelle Phan and others.

(I have a secret free resources page on my website with examples. How can you find that secret page? I'll talk about that in Chapter VIII.)

Make sure that your videos are not just viewable and watchable, but sharable. What do I mean by sharable? It is something that people want to share for "selfish" reasons, like I mentioned earlier. I also talked about this in-depth and in my other book *Digital Marketing Madness: Social Media Marketing Strategy at Super Low Cost* but the gist is people share because they are selfish.

As another example (I already gave one earlier in the chapter on "Myths versus Facts"), let's say you like golf. Have you seen a video on how to do a really good golf swing? If so, will you share it with your golf buddies? Yes, you will. Why are you sharing it; because you really want to help them? Maybe; but your real reason is that you are "selfish." You want to be "thanked and praised" for sharing it. You like it when people thank you for sharing a video. You like it when people click "like." You like it when people comment and say "thank you" to you so it makes you feel good. Why do you share a photo which is cool? It is because you want your friends to find you cool. Basically you can see it is for selfish reasons.

So the easiest way to make a "shareable" video is to make a useful instructional video which solves problems. People in your niche would generally want to share that because then their other friends will thank them for it and they'll feel good when they are thanked for it. Using this strategy, I've garnered more than 4 MILLION views on Youtube! Take note, this is not about production quality but about virality ("viral" = "virus" = contagious = people share it with each other).

Therefore, don't be paranoid about, "Oh, I don't have a good camera." "I don't have good lighting." That helps, but you don't need it. In one class I teach in social media marketing, it is often the filmmaking majors who do the WORST in making viral videos. They make these super beautiful videos which no one cares to share. Just as long as your videos are good enough and clear enough to solve people's problems, they will love you for making these videos and they will share it.

My first videos had terrible quality and even big YouTube vloggers like Michelle Phan and BubzBeauty started out with very low quality videos; but they still became big because of virality. Their videos went viral; meaning they spread and spread and spread. They were shared and re-shared because people enjoyed sharing them. So for now, just make the free videos and store it in your computer (back it up!) and upload it to YouTube later. I will talk about uploading in another step.

Step 15: Make "premium" videos.

What are premium videos? These are the videos that you are going to charge for later. They are different from your free videos because you are making the free videos to attract people and you start earning money when you charge for the premium videos that the free viewers want to upgrade to. What's a good ratio of free and premium? Well, that is up to you. Perhaps 60% free videos, 40% free videos; or 80% free, 20% premium. The most important thing is deciding which videos will be free and which videos will be premium. A common mistake is to say, "I'm going to make some good videos and some lousy videos. The lousy videos will be free and the good videos will be premium." Do NOT do that. That is a very traditional business way of thinking.

First of all, do not make any lousy videos at all, with lousy information. If you make your free videos lousy then nobody is going to share them. If nobody shares them, you will not accumulate any fans and followers. If you don't collect any followers, then nobody is going to upgrade to your premium videos. I do not recommend making your lousy videos your premium videos either because if people watch your free videos and they are great and then they pay to watch your premium videos and your premium videos suck, then people are just going to get angry. The way you divide free and premium videos is that the more general videos which will be appreciated by a greater number of people will go into the "free" column.

That's what you throw out there that lots of people will like, so people will enjoy and re-share it so that you end up with a big customer base. Your premium videos, on the other hand, would be your more detailed, "deeper" videos. These videos will be for the diehard people who really want to get deep within your niche. They are also the ones who would appreciate and be willing to pay for your premium videos.

Another important note about your free videos: you should NOT create misleading "free trap" videos in which you create "incomplete" videos which then suddenly force your customers to pay in order to see the "whole thing." Doing that is a "quick buck" scheme which is extremely irritating and will make your viewers angry. As a result, they will NOT share your free videos and you will not grow your fans and followers. No fans and followers means no one to buy your premium videos for the long term. If this is your way of doing business, then you definitely do not understand the concept of social media marketing and virality.

If you do upload any incomplete videos, they should be a minority; and **you should honestly label them as "preview" videos** so that the viewer knows what to expect and he or she is not shocked when he or she realizes the video is incomplete.

So to sum up: what exactly do you do in this step? You make the premium videos and you save them. Do not upload them anywhere yet. I will talk about uploading them in a later step.

Step 16: Create a free e-book.

Start with writing a free e-book related to your niche. It is as simple as writing it on Microsoft Word and saving it as a PDF file; but do **not** save it as a PDF yet because you will have to edit it later before you actually publish it. I am saying this early but you will see in one of the later steps on why this is so. You also have to design a nice cover for your e-book. How do you do that? Is it difficult? Nope. Have you seen those really nice e-book covers online? They are not expensive. You can have a nice e-book cover designed for as low as $5. How? You can go to Fiverr.com and you look for a reliable and honest seller who is willing to design your e-book cover for $5.

What is Fiverr.com? Fiverr.com is an amazing website. It is kind of like an eBay of online services where you can find people willing to do all sorts of services for you online for $5.

Step 17: Make a premium e-book for your niche.

Again, how do you choose what information goes into your free e-book and what information goes into your premium e-book? It is the same with the free and premium videos. You reserve the deeper, more detailed information for your premium e-book which you will sell to paying customers.

Just as in the last step, you just write one and you don't publish it yet. I will tell you when to publish it in a later step.

Step 18: Upload, embed and protect your premium videos on your website

(This step assumes your website is already up. But if it isn't yet, no worries). Embed and protect your premium videos on your website from the public using WishList Member. Do not market these premium videos yet. We'll do that in a later step.

Step 19: Hook up (I.T. speak: "integrate") your premium videos to your PayPal Premier or Business account using WishList Member "integration."

This is a bit technical, I'm sorry about that; but it's easier than you think when you follow Wishlist Member's instructional video. You do this step so that later, you can earn money when people pay to be premium members so they can watch your premium videos. When customers on your website pay via WishList Member, the money will go directly into your PayPal account.

When you have enough money in your Paypal account, you can transfer it to your bank account.

When you are choosing a price for your premium videos, makes sure you choose a price which communicates quality and value. When I say "value" I don't mean cheap. Cheap does not sell well with specialized videos and I said earlier that your premium videos and your premium e-book is about specialized, more detailed and deeper material. Do NOT believe traditional economics regarding the "Law of Supply and Demand" (which states that cheaper stuff will sell more). I have experienced it myself selling both cheap and expensive. Well, guess what? Selling cheap did NOT sell more. It sold a lot, lot less.

If you sell cheap, then your customers will compare your premium videos to free ones available online; and of course they will choose free. There is a concept in marketing called a "reassuring price" which means that people are more confident in the quality of what they are buying if the price reflects what it's worth. I am not saying you should overprice your videos; but I am saying that you should keep this in mind when you are doing your pricing. Moreover, I find that customers are not willing to go through the "hassle" of registering and typing in their credit card information for a low value (i.e. cheap) product.

Step 20: Create a sales page for your premium videos.

When you're ready to invite fans to upgrade to your premium videos, you will send them to this sales page where they can be presented with your premium offer. How do you make a sales page for your premium videos? You have to do this with your web designer or by yourself using Optimize Press or Instapage.

(I have a secret page on my website with free resources and information to help you to do this step. How can you find that secret page? I'll talk about that in Chapter VIII.)

Step 21: Upload your free videos to YouTube but keep these **unlisted** in the meantime.

When you are uploading to YouTube, you would have to look for a setting there where you can choose "public, private or unlisted." Keep the videos unlisted (for now).

They are unlisted in the meantime because you are not going to launch it yet for the public to watch. Why? Because your website is not ready yet. You don't want your YouTube viewers loving your videos and then going to your website and then finding a site which does not yet have the premium stuff available for them to buy or upgrade to. We'll go to that in another step.

Step 22: Give your YouTube videos nice thumbnail images.

Thumbnail images are the images people see on your video when they haven't clicked on it yet. If the images are nice, then people are more likely to click on them and watch them. WARNING: make sure the thumbnail image is directly related to the content of your video. If you just upload a beautiful or sexy thumbnail image which is not seen inside your video, your video will be considered as spam! Youtube may penalize you for that or even delete your video. NOTE: If you are just starting out, Youtube may not allow you to upload your own thumbnail image yet. However, Youtube will "grab" some image choices from inside your video from which you can choose your thumbnail image.

Step 23: Give your YouTube videos good titles.

Do not simply give a video a cool name. You should also induce curiosity. There are so many videos on Youtube, so why would people click on your video? You have a small window of opportunity to get people to click on your video. Fortunately, Youtube seems to put newly uploaded videos on the front page results for a short time (about a week), just to see if people actually click on the new video and to measure the response (Did the viewers "like," reshare, or subscribe? How much of the video did they watch before clicking away? And other criteria...). If you can show Youtube that your videos are getting a good response, this will help in your videos' longer term search ranking and it will be more likely to come up in the search results. WARNING: NEVER pay so called social media "experts" to deliver more "likes" or "views" to your videos. These so called experts often use unscrupulous dirty ways to increase your views and likes temporarily; but Youtube can detect these tricks very effectively and will delete your videos as well as ban you.

Step 24: Give your Youtube videos good descriptions in the description box.

As for your video's description, the first sentence should be an invite to your site or should have your web address so that once people enjoy your video, they can immediately click the link which will take them directly to your site; where of course you are eventually going to sell them something. Eventually, when you already have a lot of views on YouTube, YouTube will invite you to officially become a "YouTube partner" and this will allow you to put a pop-up "annotation" right inside your video that people can click on that will take them to your website.

However, if you are still starting out, YouTube may not allow you to do this "website-linked annotation" yet; so you just put the link to your website in the first sentence of your description. After that, give a good description about what is in the video and make sure you include keywords which are related to your niche as well. You do this so that when people search for how to do a good golf swing or whatever it is they are searching for, YouTube can detect that your video matches what people are searching for so that your video can come up highly-ranked in the search results. But again, do not over-optimize. Don't just stuff your description with keywords because if you do that, it looks "spammy" to both the audience and to YouTube and YouTube will not reward you for that in the search results. They may even penalize you.

One thing I do is to simply summarize all the words you are saying in the video and then type that into the description box. Therefore, it is not just a bunch of keywords, it is a real story. But do not type out **all** the worlds in the video. Don't give away the whole house. Why? It is more to protect yourself from "scrapers" or text pirates online. With some jerk websites, all they do is they automatically "scrape" or copy the descriptions in top YouTube videos and paste it onto their blog pages as their own "blog posts" without asking you permission. In a way, they are plagiarizing your description. So in the description, if you give away everything that is in your video, it might be misused by some other guy who, in a sense, is competing with you and stealing your information. Just post a summary and that should be enough.

Step 25: Layout your free and premium videos on your site.

Make it easy for your free viewers to watch both your free videos and premium videos on your site. Use a layout which allows your free viewers to see the premium videos so they know what they are getting if they decide to upgrade. This is a good way of gently but continually advertising you premium videos to your free video viewers.

Step 26: Create a hidden sales page for your premium e-book.

When I say "hidden" I mean this sales page should not be easy to find on your website. You can use some unmemorable URL (a.k.a. web address); something like www.yoursiteABCXYZhgiyfgfynr.com/blah-blah which people wouldn't easily remember. This sales page is where you will invite your free readers to upgrade to your premium e-book. I will tell you later what to do with this hidden sales page in a future step; so just hold on as we're getting there.

Step 27: Edit your free e-book.

After readers are finished reading your free e-book, if it is great, your readers may say, "This is a great e-book, I want more." Therefore, at the end of the book, you make your offer where you invite them to check out your premium e-book. You include a clickable link (easy to do this on MS Word) which should bring them to your premium e-book's sales page which I have talked about in the last step. Also add your nicely designed e-book cover to the front of your e-book document. Now that you've added the link and nice cover, you can save your free e-book as a PDF file.

In an earlier step, I told you to write your free e-book but not to save it yet as a PDF file. Now, in this step, you're ready to save it as a PDF because you have already added the link to your premium e-book's sales page. Saving it as a PDF is as simple as using the "Save As" function on Microsoft Word and saving as a PDF instead of a document file.

Step 28: Open an account with E-junkie.com and upload your premium e-book.

E-junkie.com has a great, easy-to-use system which will accept payments from your customers and will automatically deliver your premium e-book to them. One of the main threats in selling an e-book is that people will just buy it once and then copy it and share it with all their friends. Fortunately, E-junkie has a really cool feature to protect you from this. This feature is called "PDF stamping" which makes every e-book sold unique to the buyer, so that if ever in the future you find your e-book illegally "floating around" online on pirate sites or email trails, you can identify which of your customers was the one who originally illegally shared his copy. If you choose to do so, you may sue that customer for as much at $150,000 <u>per copy</u> illegally distributed.

(I have a secret free resources page on my website with a video which will help you learn how to use E-junkie. How can you find that secret page? I'll talk about that in Chapter VIII.)

Step 29: Create a buy now button in E-junkie for your premium e-book and insert this buy now button into your premium e-book sales page.

At this point, you have already made your premium e-book sales page and as I mentioned earlier, it should still be hidden. Now it is time to insert the buy now button into that page. After that, this web page is ready to sell!

Step 30: Change your YouTube video settings to public.

Now you are ready to launch your free videos which hopefully will attract lots of people. It will attract viewers who will become your fans, friends, followers and subscribers and hopefully, a lot of them will become your customers as well.

Note that it's normal to have few viewers of your Youtube videos in the beginning. But if your videos are great, the views will gradually increase.

Step 31: (Optional) Pay Google AdWords to insert your YouTube video into other YouTube videos within your niche. If you are too impatient to wait for people to slowly start discovering your videos, you can use Google AdWords. You simply sign up using your Gmail username and input your credit card information. And then after that, you will be able to pay Google to insert your video into other people's videos. Have you seen those annoying video advertisements on Youtube which are inserted into a video and you have to wait 5 seconds before you skip it? Well, that is exactly what am I talking about. You can insert your video and if people find your video interesting, they will watch your whole video and possibly click on it so that they'll be brought to your Youtube channel.

I know that you probably have been skipping a lot of those videos after 5 seconds; but that is because very often, the video you are being shown is another video that you are not interested in at that point in time. However, if you "target" your video properly and show your video to people who have been searching for topics similar to yours, then there is big chance that the person who sees your video will watch your video and become your follower (i.e. potential customer for premium).

Step 32: Start making your Facebook fan page.

For this you need a nice cover photo and you need other images that people want to look at and people want to share. A good example of a "shareable" image is an infographic. You can create your own on Microsoft Powerpoint and "save as" a jpeg file. Or, you can pay a freelance artist or someone of Fiverr.com to do it.

You can post your YouTube videos as well and can use some free apps like the Youtube video app for Facebook, which creates a nice, big "movie screen" for your videos. With Facebook, you have a fan page so that you can upload content which you hope will become viral; that people will share and re-share. Even though you are hosting your videos on YouTube, Facebook is often a good place to share it.

How do you get your first Facebook fans? One of the best ways is to tell people about it on your YouTube videos. You can use your Youtube description or pop up box "annotation" and say "Hey, if you like this video please subscribe to our YouTube Channel and please like us on Facebook" and of course you mention your Facebook address there in your YouTube video. Another way you can get fans on Facebook is to pay Facebook to "promote page." You pay Facebook $5 or $10 or more, depending on how much "reach" you want, to promote your page to get more fans in your target niche. Facebook will take care of locating fans for your target niche for you because Facebook knows what people "like" and so they know who would probably like your fan page. Of course you will have to specify what your fan page is about; like if it is about golfing or cosmetics or something else.

You collect these fans so that you can market to them; but more importantly, you are collecting these fans for the purpose of showing your credibility. Later on, you can show that you're a credible business with good videos; and one way of showing credibility is showing that you have a lot of Facebook fans. A lot of people measure credibility this way. And when you have a lot of credibility because you have a lot of Facebook fans, then it is easier to win their trust.

When they trust you, it is easier to ask them to upgrade to your premium videos. On the other hand, if they don't trust you, they are not going to buy from you. One caveat though about Facebook is that unfortunately, the "organic" reach has been going down to as low as 1% to 5%. What do I mean by organic reach? It means that even if you have 1,000 fans and you post something on your fan page, maybe only 10 to 50 fans (1% to 5%) are going to see your post on their newsfeeds. Facebook does <u>not</u> show your post on all of your fans' newsfeeds. In the past, Facebook used to be generous with fan page owners. If a fan page posted something, all their fans would immediately see it in their newsfeeds. Over the past 2 years however, Facebook has been reducing and reducing this exposure and reach. If you post something, very few of your fans will see it unless you pay Facebook to "boost" your post. You're pushed to pay Facebook to show it to even **your own** fans (ouch!) and you pay Facebook to show it to your "friends of fans."

Having Facebook fans also helps your credibility because if your target audience already has friends who are your fans, your posts will show them that their friends are already your fans.

Step 33: Constantly evaluate, improve, and optimize!

Naturally, your business is different from mine; there's no way I would know exactly what you would have to do in this step. Here is where you have your golden opportunity to use your personal "entrepreneurial intelligence" which I spoke of earlier. You'll make mistakes or even hit failures along the way, but you can learn from them. As I told my Facebook fans on one Chinese New Year: "I wish you success but NOT luck; luck comes from chance, but success comes from YOU."

"The longer you delay building your dream, the harder it becomes to start"

So that's it! 33 realistic steps. This is very similar to what I did and it worked for me. While I can never guarantee your future success, I honestly believe you can do it too. I can tell you how it changed my life; it is great to follow your dream and earn money at the same time rather than having no choice but to wake up for work every day and build someone else's dream. I can also say that it wasn't high risk like opening your dream café or bar or spa. What we learned in this book is a great way to increase your probability of success!

Wait... hold on; you want even more? **Turn the page and check out the next chapter!**

Chapter VIII: A Free Gift for You!

Throughout this whole book I keep on mentioning my "secret resources page" on my website from which you can get extra information to help you set up your own business. This is a page exclusive only for purchasers of my book.

So how do you find this "secret" page? Simple! I'll give you the secret web address. All I ask is you do a little something for me, and "share the love" of this book:

1) Write even just a 1 to 3 sentence honest "online review" for this book from the online

bookstore where you bought this (or if you bought this book at a traditional store, post your review on Goodreads.com). For your review name, use the same or similar name as the receipt which you got when you purchased this book.

2) Forward your email receipt (or photo of real receipt) for this book to BookBuyer@Entrepreneurgasm.com indicating where you posted your review (make sure you do NOT expose your full/complete credit card number).

3) I'll quickly check to see that your online review name matches with your receipt name and I'll immediately send you the link to my secret resources page.

Yes, it's that simple! So what are you waiting for? I look forward to sending you the link to my SECRET resources page ASAP. Cheers!

David

ABOUT THE AUTHOR

With very little capital investment and almost zero marketing expense, David Michael Ledesma built a modest but fast-growing online business with most of his customers coming from the United States and United Kingdom.

Despite starting the business just a short while back, his viral videos on YouTube have garnered more than 4 MILLION views worldwide. Being "cash flow positive" since the 6th month of operation, the startup has *never* needed any form of debt or "venture capital funding."

Due to its online nature, David's business takes up very little of his time, so he now just enjoys a relaxed, laid-back life in sunny Southeast Asia where he sometimes lectures at university. His entrepreneurial philosophy is that "if you must always work more to earn more, then there's something wrong with your business model."

www.ingramcontent.com/pod-product-compliance
Lightning Source LLC
Chambersburg PA
CBHW051810170526
45167CB00005B/1949